HAL•LEONARD

JAZZ PLAY-ALONG

Book and CD for B♭, E♭, C and Bass Clef Instruments

volume 146

RAMSEY LEWIS

Arranged and Produced by
Mark Taylor and Jim Roberts

BOOK

T0088325

CD

Cover photo © TedWilliams, CTSIMAGES

ISBN 978-1-4584-1747-3

HAL•LEONARD
CORPORATION

7777 W. BLUEMOUND RD. P.O. BOX 13819 MILWAUKEE, WI 53213

Visit Hal Leonard Online at
www.halleonard.com

RAMSEY LEWIS

Volume 146

Arranged and Produced by
Mark Taylor and Jim Roberts

Featured Players:

Graham Breedlove–Trumpet
John Desalme–Tenor Sax
Tony Nalker–Piano
Regan Brough–Bass
Jim Roberts–Guitar
Todd Harrison–Drums

**Recorded at Bias Studios, Springfield, Virginia
Bob Dawson, Engineer**

HOW TO USE THE CD:

Each song has <u>two</u> tracks:

1) Split Track/Melody

Woodwind, Brass, Keyboard, and **Mallet Players** can use this track as a learning tool for melody style and inflection.

Bass Players can learn and perform with this track – remove the recorded bass track by turning down the volume on the LEFT channel.

Keyboard and **Guitar Players** can learn and perform with this track – remove the recorded piano part by turning down the volume on the RIGHT channel.

2) Full Stereo Track

Soloists or **Groups** can learn and perform with this accompaniment track with the RHYTHM SECTION only.

BRAZILICA

CD
1 : SPLIT TRACK/MELODY
2 : FULL STEREO TRACK

C VERSION

BY MAURICE WHITE
AND MARTIN YARBOROUGH

CARMEN

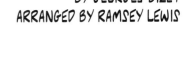

BY GEORGES BIZET
ARRANGED BY RAMSEY LEWIS

C VERSION

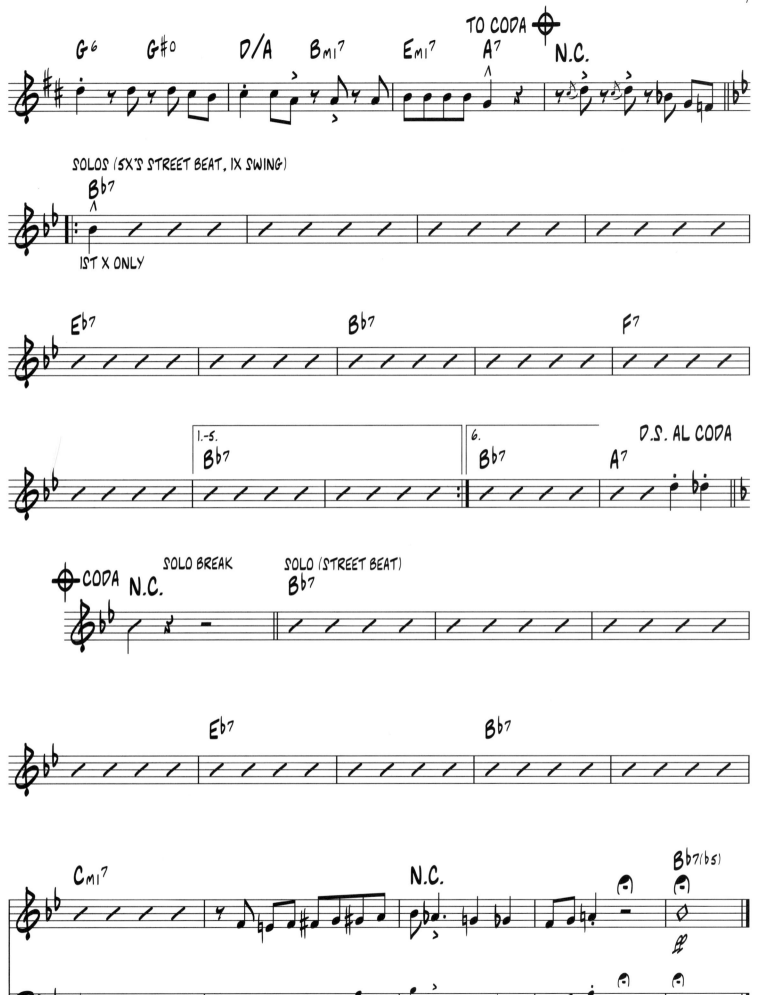

DO WHAT YOU WANNA

BY RAMSEY LEWIS

C VERSION

HANG ON SLOOPY

WORDS AND MUSIC BY WES FARRELL
AND BERT RUSSELL

THE "IN" CROWD

WORDS AND MUSIC BY
BILLY PAGE

C VERSION

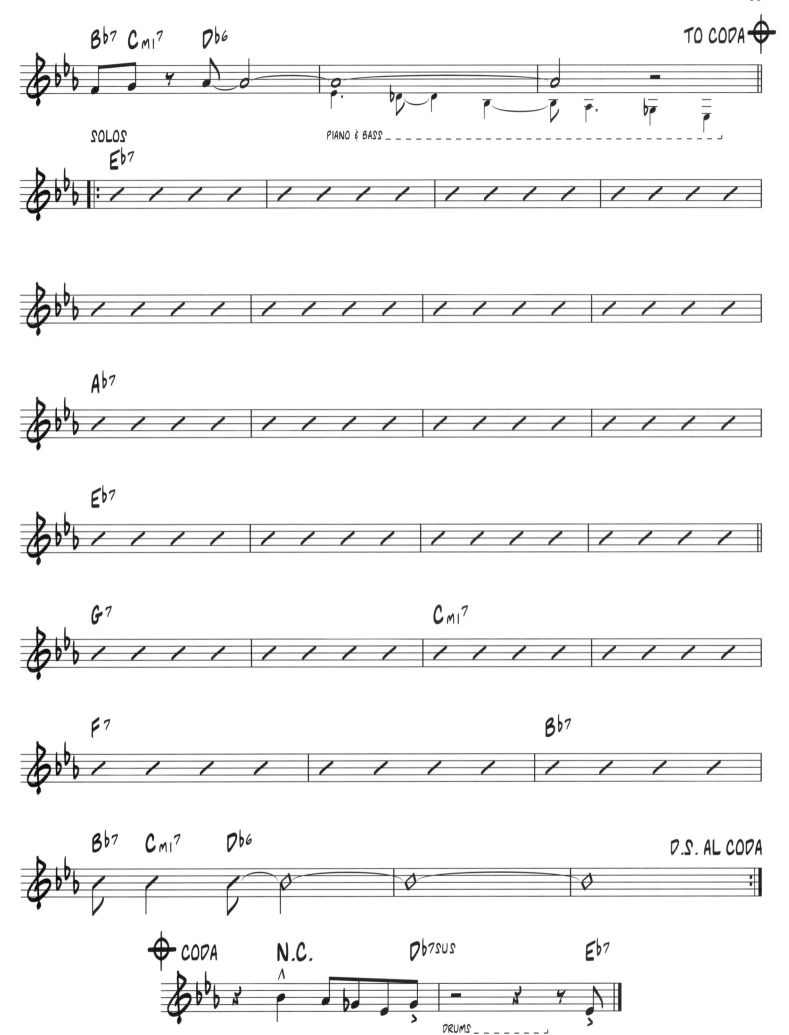

Julia

CD

11 : SPLIT TRACK/MELODY

12 : FULL STEREO TRACK

C VERSION

WORDS AND MUSIC BY JOHN LENNON
AND PAUL McCARTNEY

CD
🔷 **13** : SPLIT TRACK/MELODY
🔷 **14** : FULL STEREO TRACK

LES FLEURS

BY CHARLES STEPNEY

C VERSION

Oh Happy Day

ARRANGEMENT BY
EDWIN R. HAWKINS

C VERSION

CD

WADE IN THE WATER

WORDS AND MUSIC BY
RAMSEY LEWIS

C VERSION

MEDIUM ROCK

SUN GODDESS

WORDS AND MUSIC BY MAURICE WHITE
AND JON LIND

C VERSION

SUN GODDESS

WORDS AND MUSIC BY MAURICE WHITE
AND JON LIND

Bb VERSION · MEDIUM FUNK

BRAZILICA

BY MAURICE WHITE
AND MARTIN YARBOROUGH

Bb VERSION

CARMEN

CD
3 : SPLIT TRACK/MELODY
4 : FULL STEREO TRACK

BY GEORGES BIZET
ARRANGED BY RAMSEY LEWIS

Bb VERSION

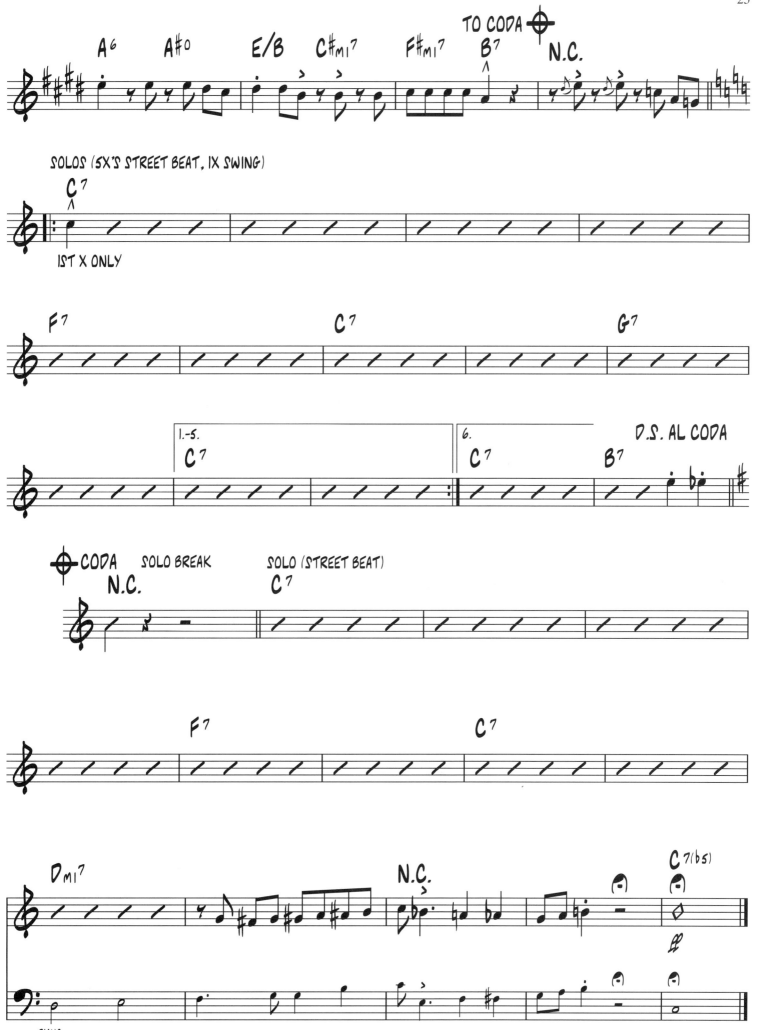

DO WHAT YOU WANNA

BY RAMSEY LEWIS

Hang On Sloopy

WORDS AND MUSIC BY WES FARRELL
AND BERT RUSSELL

THE "IN" CROWD

WORDS AND MUSIC BY
BILLY PAGE

CD
9: SPLIT TRACK/MELODY
10: FULL STEREO TRACK

Bb VERSION

JULIA

WORDS AND MUSIC BY JOHN LENNON
AND PAUL McCARTNEY

Bb VERSION

CD
🔷13 : SPLIT TRACK/MELODY
🔷14 : FULL STEREO TRACK

LES FLEURS

BY CHARLES STEPNEY

Bb VERSION

OH HAPPY DAY

ARRANGEMENT BY
EDWIN R. HAWKINS

WADE IN THE WATER

WORDS AND MUSIC BY
RAMSEY LEWIS

Bb VERSION

BRAZILICA

BY MAURICE WHITE
AND MARTIN YARBOROUGH

Eb VERSION

CARMEN

BY GEORGES BIZET
ARRANGED BY RAMSEY LEWIS

CD
- **3** : SPLIT TRACK/MELODY
- **4** : FULL STEREO TRACK

Eb VERSION

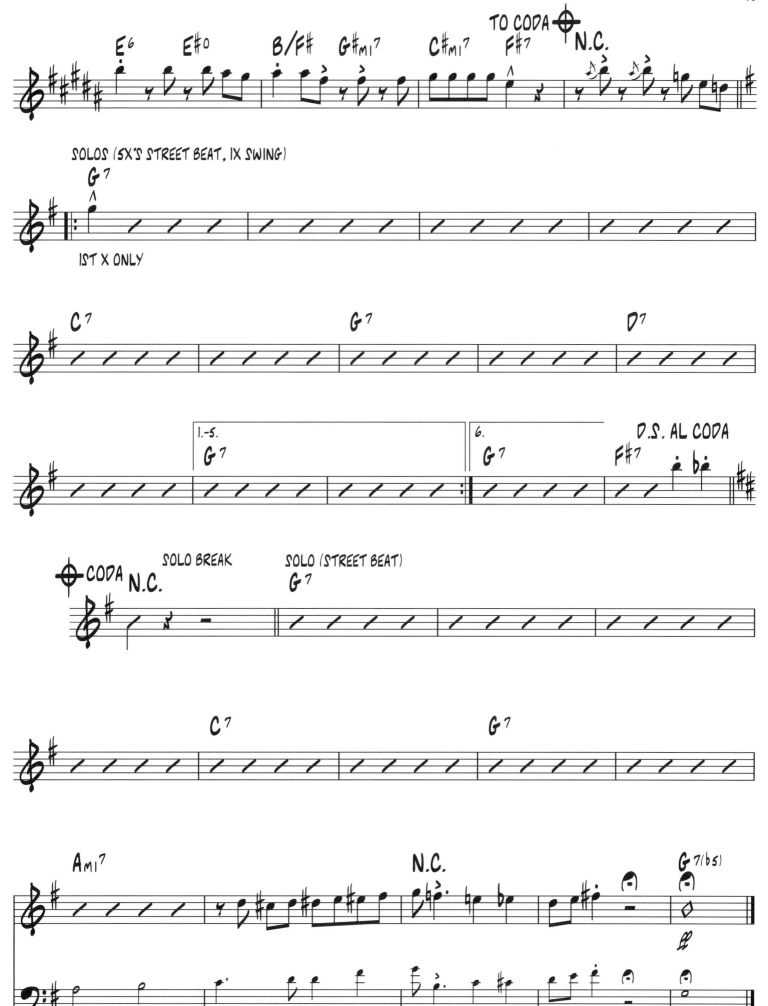

HANG ON SLOOPY

WORDS AND MUSIC BY WES FARRELL
AND BERT RUSSELL

Eb VERSION

THE "IN" CROWD

CD
9: SPLIT TRACK/MELODY
10: FULL STEREO TRACK

WORDS AND MUSIC BY
BILLY PAGE

Eb VERSION

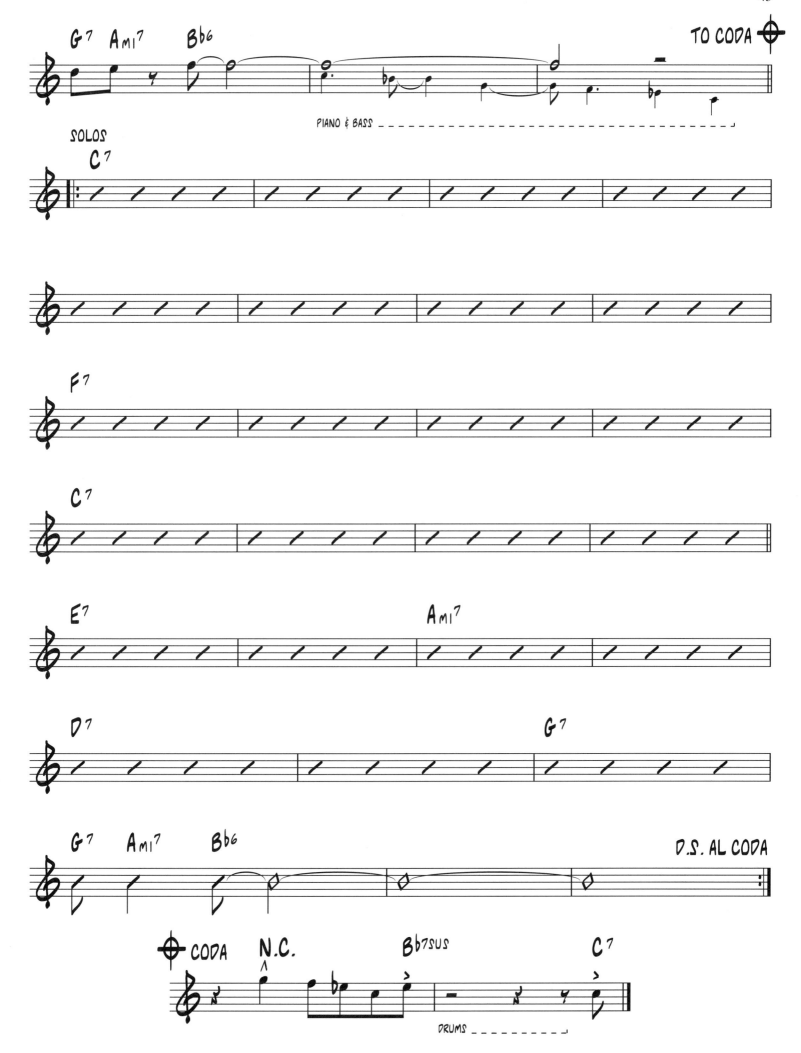

JULIA

WORDS AND MUSIC BY JOHN LENNON
AND PAUL McCARTNEY

Eb VERSION

CD

LES FLEURS

BY CHARLES STEPNEY

Eb VERSION

MEDIUM LATIN

OH HAPPY DAY

15 : SPLIT TRACK/MELODY
16 : FULL STEREO TRACK

ARRANGEMENT BY
EDWIN R. HAWKINS

Eb VERSION

CD
19 : SPLIT TRACK/MELODY
20 : FULL STEREO TRACK

WADE IN THE WATER

WORDS AND MUSIC BY
RAMSEY LEWIS

Eb VERSION

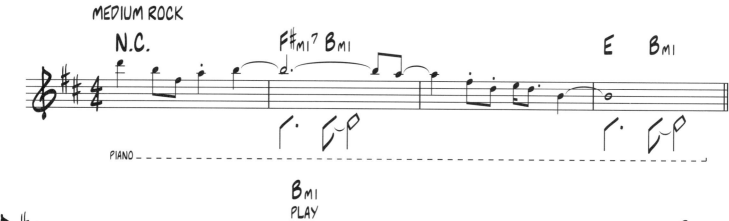

SUN GODDESS

WORDS AND MUSIC BY MAURICE WHITE
AND JON LIND

CD
🔷17 : SPLIT TRACK/MELODY
🔷18 : FULL STEREO TRACK

SUN GODDESS

WORDS AND MUSIC BY MAURICE WHITE
AND JON LIND

𝄢: C VERSION

MEDIUM FUNK

F7SUS

GUITAR - - - - - -

Eb7SUS

F7SUS   Eb7SUS   PLAY

+PIANO -   mf

𝄋 BbMA7   Gmi7   Ami7   C7SUS   C#7SUS

Emi7(b5)   A+7(b9)   Dmi7   G7   Cmi7

Gmi7   ⌐1. F7SUS   ⌐2. Cmi7   Gmi7

Cmi7   Gmi7   TO CODA ⊕   SOLOS (PLAY 3X'S)   D.S. AL CODA
                             F7SUS   Eb7SUS   TAKE 2ND ENDING

⊕ CODA   F7SUS   Eb7SUS   F7SUS

BRAZILICA

BY MAURICE WHITE
AND MARTIN YARBOROUGH

𝄢: C VERSION

MEDIUM FUNK

CD

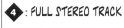

CARMEN

BY GEORGES BIZET
ARRANGED BY RAMSEY LEWIS

C VERSION — BRIGHT LATIN

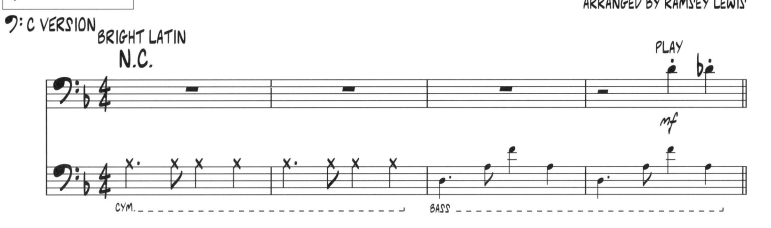

DO WHAT YOU WANNA

BY RAMSEY LEWIS

HANG ON SLOOPY

WORDS AND MUSIC BY WES FARRELL
AND BERT RUSSELL

THE "IN" CROWD

WORDS AND MUSIC BY
BILLY PAGE

CD

9 : SPLIT TRACK/MELODY
10 : FULL STEREO TRACK

𝄢: C VERSION

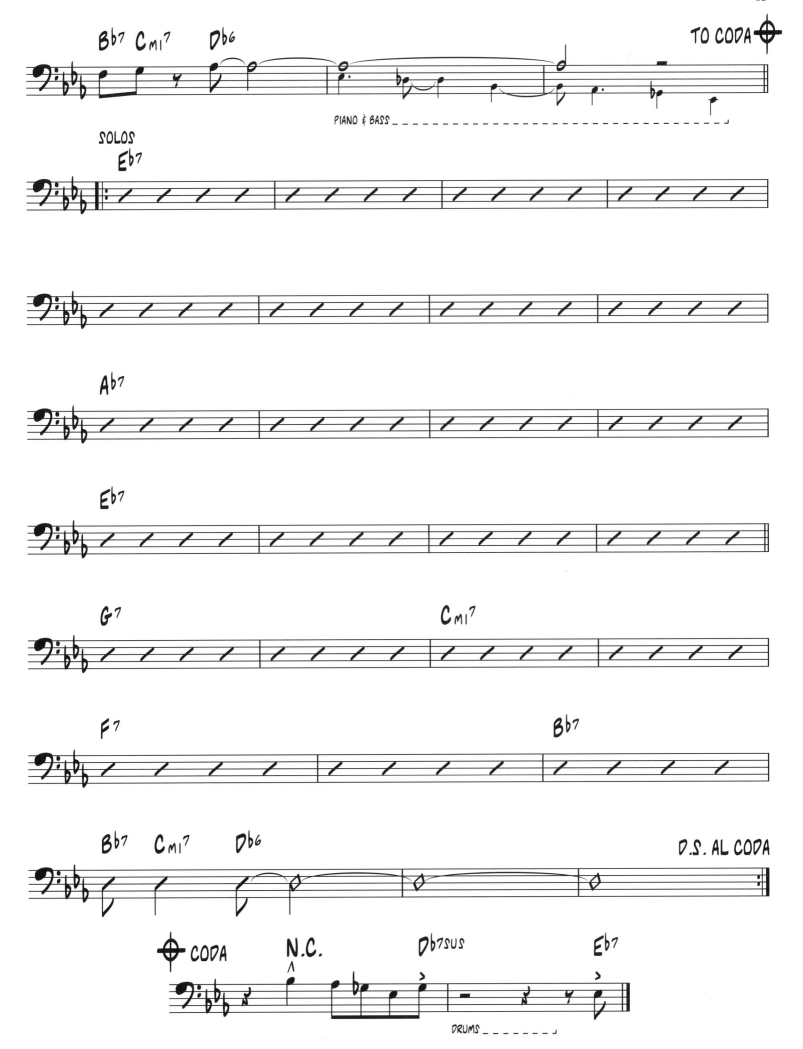

CD

11 : SPLIT TRACK/MELODY
12 : FULL STEREO TRACK

JULIA

WORDS AND MUSIC BY JOHN LENNON
AND PAUL McCARTNEY

🎵: C VERSION

MEDIUM BALLAD

LES FLEURS

BY CHARLES STEPNEY

OH HAPPY DAY

ARRANGEMENT BY
EDWIN R. HAWKINS

🎵: C VERSION

WADE IN THE WATER

WORDS AND MUSIC BY
RAMSEY LEWIS

Presenting the Hal Leonard JAZZ PLAY-ALONG® SERIES

For use with all B-flat, E-flat, Bass Clef and C instruments, the Jazz Play-Along® Series is the ultimate learning tool for all jazz musicians. With musician-friendly lead sheets, melody cues, and other split-track choices on the included CD, these first-of-a-kind packages help you master improvisation while playing some of the greatest tunes of all time. FOR STUDY, each tune includes a split track with: melody cue with proper style and inflection • professional rhythm tracks • choruses for soloing • removable bass part • removable piano part. FOR PERFORMANCE, each tune also has: an additional full stereo accompaniment track (no melody) • additional choruses for soloing.

1A. MAIDEN VOYAGE/ALL BLUES
00843158 .... $15.99

1. DUKE ELLINGTON
00841644 .... $16.95

2. MILES DAVIS
00841645 .... $16.95

3. THE BLUES
00841646 .... $16.99

4. JAZZ BALLADS
00841691 .... $16.99

5. BEST OF BEBOP
00841689 .... $16.95

6. JAZZ CLASSICS WITH EASY CHANGES
00841690 .... $16.99

7. ESSENTIAL JAZZ STANDARDS
00843000 .... $16.99

8. ANTONIO CARLOS JOBIM AND THE ART OF THE BOSSA NOVA
00843001 .... $16.95

9. DIZZY GILLESPIE
00843002 .... $16.99

10. DISNEY CLASSICS
00843003 .... $16.99

11. RODGERS AND HART FAVORITES
00843004 .... $16.99

12. ESSENTIAL JAZZ CLASSICS
00843005 .... $16.99

13. JOHN COLTRANE
00843006 .... $16.95

14. IRVING BERLIN
00843007 .... $15.99

15. RODGERS & HAMMERSTEIN
00843008 .... $15.99

16. COLE PORTER
00843009 .... $15.95

17. COUNT BASIE
00843010 .... $16.95

18. HAROLD ARLEN
00843011 .... $15.95

19. COOL JAZZ
00843012 .... $15.95

20. CHRISTMAS CAROLS
00843080 .... $14.95

21. RODGERS AND HART CLASSICS
00843014 .... $14.95

22. WAYNE SHORTER
00843015 .... $16.95

23. LATIN JAZZ
00843016 .... $16.95

24. EARLY JAZZ STANDARDS
00843017 .... $14.95

25. CHRISTMAS JAZZ
00843018 .... $16.95

26. CHARLIE PARKER
00843019 .... $16.95

27. GREAT JAZZ STANDARDS
00843020 .... $16.99

28. BIG BAND ERA
00843021 .... $15.99

29. LENNON AND MCCARTNEY
00843022 .... $16.95

30. BLUES' BEST
00843023 .... $15.99

31. JAZZ IN THREE
00843024 .... $15.99

32. BEST OF SWING
00843025 .... $15.99

33. SONNY ROLLINS
00843029 .... $15.95

34. ALL TIME STANDARDS
00843030 .... $15.99

35. BLUESY JAZZ
00843031 .... $16.99

36. HORACE SILVER
00843032 .... $16.99

37. BILL EVANS
00843033 .... $16.95

38. YULETIDE JAZZ
00843034 .... $16.95

39. "ALL THE THINGS YOU ARE" & MORE JEROME KERN SONGS
00843035 .... $15.99

40. BOSSA NOVA
00843036 .... $16.99

41. CLASSIC DUKE ELLINGTON
00843037 .... $16.99

42. GERRY MULLIGAN FAVORITES
00843038 .... $16.99

43. GERRY MULLIGAN CLASSICS
00843039 .... $16.99

44. OLIVER NELSON
00843040 .... $16.95

45. JAZZ AT THE MOVIES
00843041 .... $15.99

46. BROADWAY JAZZ STANDARDS
00843042 .... $15.99

47. CLASSIC JAZZ BALLADS
00843043 .... $15.99

48. BEBOP CLASSICS
00843044 .... $16.99

49. MILES DAVIS STANDARDS
00843045 .... $16.95

50. GREAT JAZZ CLASSICS
00843046 .... $15.99

51. UP-TEMPO JAZZ
00843047 .... $15.99

52. STEVIE WONDER
00843048 .... $16.99

53. RHYTHM CHANGES
00843049 .... $15.99

54. "MOONLIGHT IN VERMONT" AND OTHER GREAT STANDARDS
00843050 .... $15.99

55. BENNY GOLSON
00843052 .... $15.95

56. "GEORGIA ON MY MIND" & OTHER SONGS BY HOAGY CARMICHAEL
00843056 .... $15.99

57. VINCE GUARALDI
00843057 .... $16.99

58. MORE LENNON AND MCCARTNEY
00843059 .... $16.99

59. SOUL JAZZ
00843060 .... $16.99

60. DEXTER GORDON
00843061 .... $15.95

61. MONGO SANTAMARIA
00843062 .... $15.95

62. JAZZ-ROCK FUSION
00843063 .... $16.99